Asynchronous JavaScript

Amin Meyghani

Asynchronous JavaScript

Amin Meyghani

January 9, 2018

Contents

Preface

The asynchronous nature of JavaScript is one of the aspects of the language that can confuse a lot of people. Having a good understanding of its primary async constructs however can reduce a lot of confusion about the language. The goal of this book is to introduce you to async programming in JavaScript and provide you with the necessary techniques to write clean and maintainable async code. We will start by exploring synchronous and asynchronous execution models and their differences. Then we'll dive into callback functions and examine how they are used to capture results of async operations. After that, we'll explore promises and learn how they abstract callback functions to simplify async flows. And at the end we'll explore `async` functions and illustrate how they can be used along with promises to further simplify asynchronous operations.

Book Outline

Chapter 1: Introduction focuses on the async model in JavaScript. It explores the key differences between async and synchronous models

Chapter 2: Callbacks describes what callbacks are and how they are used to capture results of async operations

Chapter 3: Promises introduces promises and how they can be used to manage async operations

Chapter 4: Async Await explores the asycn/await abstraction around generators and promises and how they can be used to simplify async flows

Using the Project Files

All the source code and project files are available on Github: https://github.com/aminmeyghani/asyncjs-book. You can simply clone the repository and run the code snippets included in the `code` directory. Alternatively you can download the repository as a zip file. If you have any feedback or find any issues with the book you can create an issue on the Github repository. Just make sure to use an appropriate tag for the issue that you create.

Requirements

This book assumes that you know the basics of JavaScript and Node. All the code snippets assumes a unix-like environment. If you are on Windows you may wanna try something like Cygwin to get a unix-like environment.

Book Updates

This book will be periodically updated with new chapters and exercises. Make sure to join the slack channel at https://asyncjsbook.now.sh to get updates and discuss what you want to see next in the book.

1 Introduction

If you are new to async programming in JavaScript, you might be surprised with the result of the following piece of code:

```
1  setTimeout(function() {
2    console.log('1');
3  }, 0);
4  console.log('2');
```

What do you think the output of the above code will be? You might be tempted to say 1 and then 2, but the correct answer is 2 and then 1. In th following sections we will dive into the asynchronous model used in JavaScript and explain why the above code prints 2 and then 1.

1.1 Synchronous vs Asynchronous

When you do your daily tasks it's highly likely that you do them asynchronously. Let's look at an analogy to illustrate the difference between the synchronous and asynchronous models of execution.

Imagine that you have three tasks to do in your daily chores list:

1. Do laundry
2. Do groceries
3. Cook dinner

With a synchronous model, you have to finish each task before moving on to the next. That is, you have to finish laundry first before moving onto doing the groceries. If your laundry machine is broken, you cannot do the groceries. The same applies for the third task, you can only cook dinner if and only if you have completed the groceries (and laundry).

Now with an asynchronous model, you don't have to wait for each task to finish to move onto the next. You can start the washing machine and do the groceries while your clothes are being washed. By the time you come back from the grocery store, your clothes are washed. Now if you need to dry your clothes, you can put them in the dryer and cook dinner while your clothes are being dried.

That's basically the main difference between the synchronous and asynchronous models of execution. In the synchronous model, you have to wait for each task to finish before moving onto the next. But in the asynchronous model you don't have to. You can schedule tasks in a way to effectively do more in less time and not wait if you don't have to. In the next section we will look at the event loop and learn how JavaScript deals with asynchronous tasks.

1.2 The Event Loop

Let's look at the snippet that we saw in the beginning of the chapter:

```
1  setTimeout(function() {
2    console.log('1');
3  }, 0);
4  console.log('2');
```

When you call the `setTimeout` method, it will be pushed on what is called the message queue. After that, the `console.log(2)` will be called immediately. After `console.log(2)` is called the stack empty and JavaScript moves onto the queue and executes what's on the queue. The mechanism that manages this flow is called the event loop. The event loop is responsible for looking at what's on the stack and the queue and scheduling the execution in the right order. In the figure below there are three tasks on the stack to be executed. Once they are finished, two more tasks are picked up from the queue and placed on he stack to be executed:

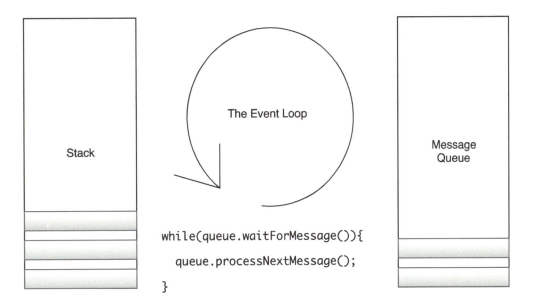

Now that's an oversimplified version of the event loop. Obviously it's way more complicated than that, but in essence, the event loop is responsible for listening for tasks that can be executed in the near future.

2   Callback Functions

Before talking about callback functions in an async context, it's important to learn how functions can be passed to other functions. Let's look at an example and see how functions can be passed around just like any value in JavaScript.

```
1  var name = 'Tom';
2  hello(name);
```

In the code snippet above we define a variable called name and we assign a string to it. Then we pass it to the hello function as an argument. We can do the exact same thing with a function. We can define name to be a function instead and pass it to hello:

```
1  function name() {
2    return 'Tom';
3  }
4  hello(name);
```

Technically speaking name is a callback function because it's passed to another function, but let's see what a callback function is in the context of an asynchronous operation.

In an async context, a callback function is just a normal JavaScript function that is called by JavaScript when an asynchronous operation is finished. By convention, a callback function usually takes two arguments. The first captures errors, and the second captures the results. A callback function can be named or anonymous, but it's better to name them. Let's look at a simple example showing how to read the content of a file asynchronously using Node's `fs.readFile` method:

```
1  function handleReading(error, result) {
2    console.log(result);
3  }
4  fs.readFile('./my-file.txt', handleReading);
```

The `fs` module has a method called `readFile`. It takes two required arguments, the first is the path to the file, and the second a callback function. In the snippet above, the callback function is `handleReading` that takes two arguments. The first captures potential errors and the second captures the content.

Below is another example from the `https` module for making a `GET` request to a remote API server:

code/callbacks/http-example.js

```
1   const https = require('https');
2   const url = 'https://jsonplaceholder.typicode.com/posts/1';
3
4   https.get(url, function(response) {
5     response.setEncoding('utf-8');
6     let body = '';
7     response.on('data', (d) => {
8       body += d;
9     });
10    response.on('end', (x) => {
11      console.log(body);
12    });
13  });
```

When you call the get method, a request is scheduled by JavaScript. When the result is available, JavaScript will call our function and will provide us with the result.

2.1 "Returning" an Async Result

When you perform an async operation, you cannot simply use the return statement to get the result. Let's say you have a function that wraps an async call. If you create a variable, and set it in the async callback, you won't be able to get the result from the outer function by simply returning the value:

```
1   function getData(options) {
2     var finalResult;
3     asyncTask(options, function(err, result) {
4       finalResult = result;
5     })
6     return finalResult;
7   }
8   getData(); // -> returns undefined
```

In the snippet above, when you call getData, it is immediately executed and the returned value is undefined. That's because at the time of calling the function, finalResult is not set to anything. It's only after a later point in time that the value gets set. The correct way of wrapping an async call, is to pass the outer function a callback:

```
1  function getData(options, callback) {
2    asyncTask(options, callback);
3  }
4  getData({}, function(err, result) {
5    if(err) return console.log(err);
6    console.log(result);
7  });
```

In the snippet above, we define **getData** to accept a callback function as the second argument. We have also named it callback to make it clear that **getData** expects a callback function as its second argument.

2.2   Async Tasks In-order

If you have a couple of async tasks that depend on each other, you will have to call each task within the other task's callback. For example, if you need to copy the content of a file, you would need to read the content of the file first before writing it to another file. Because of that you would need to call the **writeFile** method within the **readFile** callback:

```
1  const fs = require('fs');
2  fs.readFile('file.txt', 'utf-8', function readContent(err, content) {
3    if(err) {
4      return console.log(err);
5    }
6    fs.writeFile('copy.txt', content, function(err) {
7      if(err) {
8        return console.log(err);
9      }
10     return console.log('done');
11   });
12 });
```

Now, it could get messy if you have a lot of async operations that depend on each other. In that case, it's better to name each callback function and define them separately to avoid confusion:

```
1  const fs = require('fs');
2  fs.readFile('file.txt', 'utf-8', readCb);
3
```

```
4  function readCb(err, content) {
5    if (err) {
6      return console.log(err);
7    }
8    return fs.writeFile('copy.txt', content, writeCb);
9  }
10
11 function writeCb(err) {
12   if(err) {
13     return console.log(err);
14   }
15   return console.log('Done');
16 }
```

In the snippet above we have defined two callback functions separately, readCb and writeCb. The benefits might not be that obvious from the example above, but for operations that have multiple dependencies, the named callback functions can save you a lot of hair-pulling down the line.

3 Promises

A promise is an object that represents the result of an asynchronous operation that may or may not succeed when executed at some point in the future. For example, when you make a request to an API server, you can return a promise that would represent the result of the api call. The api call may or may not succeed, but eventually you will get a promise object that you can use. The function below performs an api call and returns the result in the form of a promise:

code/promises/axios-example.js

```
1  const axios = require('axios');
2  function getDataFromServer() {
3    const result =  axios.get('https://jsonplaceholder.typicode.com/posts/1');
4    return result;
5  }
```

- On line 1, we load the axios module which is a promise-based http client
- On line 3, we make a GET request to a public api endpoint and store the result in the `result` constant
- On line 4, we return the promise

Now, we can simply call the function and access the results and catch possible errors:

```
1  getDataFromServer()
2    .then(function(response) {
3      console.log(response);
4    })
5    .catch(function(error) {
6      console.log(error);
7    });
```

Every promise has a **then** and a **catch** method. You would use the **then** method to capture the result of the operation if it succeeds (resolved promise), and the **catch** method if the operation fails (rejected promise). Note that both **then** and **catch** receive a callback function with a single argument to capture the result. Also, it's worth noting that both of these methods return a promise that allows us to potentially chain more promises.

Below are a couple of other examples of asynchronous tasks that can return a promise:

11

- Reading the content of a file: the promise returned will include the content of the file
- Listing the content of a directory: the promise returned will include the list of files
- Parsing a csv file: the promise returned will include the parsed content
- Running some query against a database to get some result

The figure below summaries the states that a promise can have:

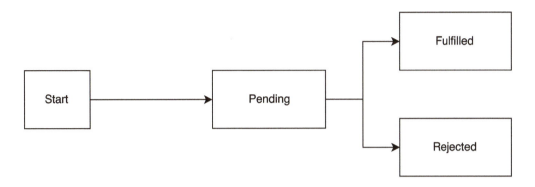

3.1 Promise Advantages

Promises existed in other languages and were introduced to JavaScript to provide an abstraction over the callback mechanism. Callbacks are the primary mechanisms for dealing with asynchronous tasks, but they can get tedious to work with. Promises were implemented in JavaScript to simplify working with callbacks and asynchronous tasks. There are many articles out there about callback hassles, just google "callback hell in JavaScript" and the results won't disappoint you.

3.2 Making a Promise

We can create a promise using the global **Promise** constructor:

```
1  const myPromise = new Promise();
```

The promise constructor takes a callback function with two arguments. The first argument is used to resolve or capture the result of an asynchronous operation, and the second is used to capture errors:

```
1  const myPromise = new Promise(function(resolve, reject) {
2    if(someError) {
```

```
3      reject(new Error(someError));
4    } else {
5      resolve('ok');
6    }
7  });
```

And as mentioned before, we can use the **then** method to use the results when the promise is resolved, and the **catch** method to handle errors:

```
1  myPromise
2    .then(function(result) {
3      console.log(result);
4    })
5    .catch(function(error) {
6      console.log(error);
7    });
```

It's worth mentioning that we can wrap any asynchronous operation in a promise. For example, the **fs.readFile** is an method that reads the content of a file asynchronously. The **fs.readFile** method is used as follows:

```
1  fs.readFile('some-file.txt', 'utf-8', function(error, content) {
2    if(error) {
3      return console.log(error);
4    }
5    console.log(content);
6  });
```

We can create a function called **readFile** that uses **fs.readFile**, reads the content of a file and resolves a promise with the content, or reject it if there is an error:

code/promises/wrap-readfile1.js

```
1  const fs = require('fs');
2  function readFile(file, format) {
3    format = format || 'utf-8';
4    function handler(resolve, reject) {
5      fs.readFile(file, format, function(err, content) {
```

```
6      if(err) {
7          return reject(err);
8      }
9      return resolve(content);
10     });
11  }
12  const promise = new Promise(handler);
13  return promise;
14 }
```

The same code can be re written more concisely as follows:

code/promises/wrap-readfile2.js

```
1  const fs = require('fs');
2  function readFile(file, format = 'utf-8') {
3    return new Promise((resolve, reject) => {
4      fs.readFile(file, format, (err, content) => {
5        if(err) return reject(err);
6        resolve(content);
7      });
8    });
9  }
```

Now we can simply call our function and capture the result in the then method, and catch errors using the catch method:

```
1  readFile('./example.txt')
2    .then(content => console.log(content))
3    .catch(err => console.log(err));
```

Even more concisely we can re write the code above using the util.promisify method that was introduced in Node 8:

code/promises/promisify-example.js

```
1  const fs = require('fs');
2  const util = require('util');
```

```
3  const readFile = util.promisify(fs.readFile);

4

5  readFile('./example.txt', 'utf-8')
6    .then(content => console.log(content))
7    .catch(err => console.log(err));
```

The `util.promisify` method takes a function that follows the Node callback convention and returns a promise-based version. You may be wondering why doesn't node make all the methods promise-based. Low level Node methods are not promise based because promises are higher level abstractions over callbacks. It's up to the programmer to decide whether or not they need a higher abstraction like promises to handle async operations.

3.3   Promise Static Methods

The `Promise` constructor has a couple of useful static methods that is worth exploring. All the code snippets are in `code/promises/static-methods.js`. Some notable ones are listed below:

`Promise.resolve`: a shortcut for creating a promise object resolved with a given value

```
1  function getData() {
2    return Promise.resolve('some data');
3  }
4  getData()
5    .then(d => console.log(d));
```

`Promise.reject`: a shortcut for creating a promise object rejected with a given value

```
1  function rejectPromise() {
2    return Promise.reject(new Error('something went wrong'));
3  }
4  rejectPromise()
5    .catch(e => console.log(e));
```

`Promise.all`: used to wait for a couple of promises to be resolved

```
1  const p1 = Promise.resolve('v1');
2  const p2 = Promise.resolve('v2');
3  const p3 = Promise.resolve('v3');
```

```
4
5  const all = Promise.all([p1, p2, p3]);
6
7  all.then(values => console.log(values[0], values[1], values[2]));
```

Note that `Promise.all` takes an array of promise objects and "waits" until all of them are resolved. Eventually it will return a promise object that contains all the values in an array in the order that they were submitted.

3.4 Promises in a Sequence

If you want to run a couple of asynchronous tasks in a sequence, you can follow the following pattern:

```
1  const promiseChain = task1()
2    .then(function(task1Result) {
3      return task2();
4    })
5    .then(function(task2Result) {
6      return task3();
7    })
8    .then(function(task3Result){
9      return task4();
10   })
11   .then(function(task4Result) {
12     console.log('done', task4Result);
13   })
14   .catch(function(err) {
15     console.log('Error', err);
16   });
```

The promise chain is kicked off by calling the first task that returns a promise. Afterwards, the **then** method is called which also returns a promise allowing us to keep chaining the **then** calls. Let's look at an example to say how you may want to use this pattern.

Let's say we have a text file that contains a bunch of invalid characters the we need to remove. In order to accomplish that, first, we need to read the content of the file. Then, we need to remove the invalid characters, and finally write the results to another file. Assuming that we have a function for each operation that returns a promise, we can define the following promise chain:

```
1  const promiseChain = readFile('example.txt')
2    .then(function(content) {
3      return removeInvalidChracters(content);
4    })
5    .then(function(cleanContent) {
6      return writeToFile('./clean-file.txt', cleanContent);
7    })
8    .then(function() {
9      console.log('done');
10   })
11   .catch(function(error) {
12     console.log(error);
13   });
```

Using the above promise chain, each task is finished before the next one starts causing the tasks to happen "in order".

3.5 Running Promises Concurrently

When you call an asynchronous function that returns a promise, you can assume that the operation is executed asynchronously. Therefore, if you call each function one by one on each line, you are practically running each task concurrently:

```
1  function runAll() {
2    const p1 = taskA();
3    const p2 = taskB();
4    const p3 = taskC();
5  }
6
7  runAll();
```

Now, if you want to do something when all these operations are finished, you can use Promise.all:

code/promises/run-all.js

```
1  function runAll() {
2    const p1 = taskA();
3    const p2 = taskB();
4    const p3 = taskC();
5    return Promise.all([p1, p2, p3]);
6  }
7
8  runAll()
9    .then(d => console.log(d, 'all done'))
10   .catch(e => console.log(e));
```

In the next section we will explore how you can combine promises that run concurrently and promises that need to run in-order.

3.6 Combining Promises

The main motivation for this section is mainly for the type of tasks that need to run concurrently and in sequence. Let's say you have a bunch of files that you need to manipulate asynchronously. You may need to perform operation A, B, C, D in order on 3 different files, but you don't care about the order that the files are processed in. All you care about is that the operations A, B, C, and D happen in the right order. We can use the following pattern to achieve that:

1. Create a list of promises
2. Each promise represents the sequence of async tasks A, B, C, D
3. Use `Promise.all` to process all the promises. Note that the `all` method processes the promises concurrently

```
1  const files = ['a.txt', 'b.txt', 'c.txt'];
2
3  function performInOrder(file) {
4    const promise = taskA(file)
5    .then(taskB)
6    .then(taskC)
7    .then(taskD);
8    return promise;
9  }
10
11 const operations = files.map(performInOrder);
```

```
12   const result = Promise.all(operations);
13
14   result.then(d => console.log(d)).catch(e => console.log(e));
```

Below is an actual code that you can run, assuming that you have the three files `a.txt`,
`b.txt` and `c.txt`:

code/promises/read-write-multiple-files/main.js

```
1    const fs = require('fs');
2    const util = require('util');
3    const readFile = util.promisify(fs.readFile);
4    const writeFile = util.promisify(fs.writeFile);
5
6    const copyFile = (file) => (content) => (writeFile(file + '-copy.txt', content));
7    const replaceContent = input => (Promise.resolve(input.replace(/-/g, 'zzzz')));
8    const processEachInOrder = file => {
9      return readFile(file, 'utf-8')
10       .then(replaceContent)
11       .then(copyFile(file));
12   }
13
14   const files = ['./a.txt', './b.txt', './c.txt'];
15   const promises = files.map(processEachInOrder);
16   Promise.all(promises)
17     .then(d => console.log(d))
18     .catch(e => console.log(e));
```

It's worth noting that this kind of processing can introduce a big workload on the CPU if the
input size is large. A better approach would be to limit the number of tasks that are processed
concurrently. The `async` library has a qeueue method that limits the number of async tasks
that are processed at a time, reducing extra workload on the CPU. We will explore the `async`
library in later sections.

3.7   Exercise

As an exercise, write a script that reads the content of a directory (1 level deep) and copys
only the files to another directory called `output`.

19

Hint You can use the example from the previous section as a starting point

Hint Here is the general idea: read the content of the folder, use the `stat` method to figure out which entry is a file, make the output folder, read each file, and write to the output folder

3.8 Solution

Below is one possible solution that uses the `Promise.all` pattern to process the read-write promises:

code/promises/exercise/main.js

```
1   /*
2     List the content of the folder, filter out the files only
3     then copy to the output folder.
4   */
5   const fs = require('fs');
6   const path = require('path');
7   const util = require('util');
8   const readFile = util.promisify(fs.readFile);
9   const writeFile = util.promisify(fs.writeFile);
10  const readdir = util.promisify(fs.readdir);
11  const stat = util.promisify(fs.stat);
12  const mkdir = util.promisify(fs.mkdir);
13  const outputFolder = './output';
14
15  function isFile(f) {
16    return stat(f).then(d => d.isFile() ? f : '');
17  }
18
19  function filterFiles(list) {
20    return Promise.all(list.map(isFile))
21      .then(files => files.filter(v => v));
22  }
23
24  function readWrite(result) {
25    const files = result[1];
26    return Promise.all(files.map(f => {
27      return readFile(f)
28        .then(content => writeFile(path.join(outputFolder, f), content));
```

20

```javascript
29    }));
30  }
31
32  const getFiles = readdir('./').then(filterFiles);
33
34  Promise.all([mkdir(outputFolder), getFiles])
35    .then(readWrite)
36    .then(_ => console.log('done!'))
37    .catch(e => console.log(e));
```

4 Async Await

Async functions are higher level abstractions around generators and promises that can be used to simplify asynchronous flows. Any JavaScript function definition can be marked with the `async` keyword. When a function is marked as an `async` function, the returned value will always be wrapped in a promise. Consider the following simple function:

```
1  function add(a, b) {
2    return a + b;
3  }
```

We can simply mark the function as an async function by using the `async` keyword in the function definition:

```
1  async function add(a, b) {
2    return a + b;
3  }
```

Now when we call the function we will get a promise that wraps the actual value. To access the actual value we use the `then` method and read the value through the callback argument:

```
1  const result = add(1, 2);
2  result.then(function(sum) {
3    console.log(sum);
4  });
```

4.1 Await Operator

The `await` operator can only be used inside an async function. When you place the await operator behind an asynchronous operation, the execution is "paused" until the result is available. Let's say that we want to read the content of a file and wait until we have the content. Then we want to write the content to another file only after the read operation has completed. To do that we can define an async function `readWrite` that `awaits` on each task in the body of the function:

code/async-await/read-write-file.js

22

```
1  async function readWrite() {
2    const content = await readFile('./example.txt', 'utf-8');
3    const result = await writeFile('./example-copy.txt', content);
4    return result;
5  }
```

The `readWrite` function is marked **async** which means we can use the **await** operator in the function body. On line 1 we wait until reading the content of the file is finished. And then on line 2 we write to the file and then wait until it's finished. On line 3 we simply return the result of the write operation.

Now let's look at another example involving a couple of async tasks that depend on each other. Below is the summary of the order of the operations to execute:

1. Make a GET request to a public endpoint to get a post object
2. List the content of a local directory and pick the file that ends with the `.txt` extension.
3. Read the content of this file and and append it to the body of the post obtained from step 1
4. Write the result to a file locally called `final.txt`

In the snippet below you can see how each async operation is accompanied with the await operator pausing the **main** function to wait until the result is available:

code/async-await/post-body-example/main.js

```
1   async function main() {
2     const response = await axios.get('https://jsonplaceholder.typicode.com/posts/1');
3     const postBody = response.data.body;
4     const localFolderList = await readdir('.');
5     const textFiles = localFolderList.filter(onlyTextFiles);
6     const localFileContent = await readFile(textFiles[0], 'utf-8');
7     const finalResult = localFileContent + postBody;
8     const writeResult = await writeFile('./final.txt', finalResult);
9     return writeResult;
10  }
```

The code above looks synchronous, but it's actually not. Nothing else is blocked while each task is being performed. That's an important thing to remember, asynchronous code don't blocks other operations that are scheduled to be executed, resulting in a more efficient execution. Now let's take the example above one step further. Let's ask ourselves: what are the tasks that can be executed separately, and what are the tasks that absolutely need to be run in a certain order. In other words, how can we split this operation into two or more async parts? One possible option might be to split it up into two operations:

1. Read folder content, get the text file, read the content of the text file
2. Make GET request to get a post object

If you think about it, you don't need any information from the http call to read the content of the local text file. However, to read the content of the local text file, you need to first get the folder content and filter the text files. Now that we have grouped the tasks, we can use the `Promise.all` pattern that we used in the Promises chapter to perform all the tasks:

code/async-await/post-body-example/main-group.js

```
1  async function readLocalContent() {
2    const localFolderList = await readdir('.');
3    const textFiles = localFolderList.filter(onlyTextFiles);
4    const localFileContent = await readFile(textFiles[0], 'utf-8');
5    return localFileContent;
6  }
7
8  async function getPostObject() {
9    const response = await axios.get('https://jsonplaceholder.typicode.com/posts/1');
10   return response.data.body;
11 }
12
13 async function main() {
14   try {
15     const results = await Promise.all([readLocalContent(), getPostObject()]);
16     const finalContent = results[0] + results[1];
17     return writeFile('./final2.txt', finalContent);
18   } catch(e) {
19     return Promise.reject(e);
20   }
21 }
```

In the snippet above we have split up the two tasks into separate `async` functions allowing us to effectively run the two groups of tasks concurrently. In the `main` function we have used `Promise.all` to wait for both of the operations to finish and use the result to write the final content to a file.

4.2 Basic Error Handling

The interesting thing about async functions is that you can simply use a try catch block around a piece of asynchronous code and catch errors:

code/async-await/read-write-file-catch-error.js

```js
async function readWrite() {
  try {
    const content = await readFile('./example.txt', 'utf-8');
    const result = await writeFile('./example-copy.txt', content);
    return result;
  } catch (error) {
    console.log('An error happened while copying the file.');
    return Promise.reject(error);
  }
}
```

In the snippet above we wrap our async code with a try catch block. If an error happens in any of the steps, we can catch it and return a rejected promise. In later chapters we'll dive deeper into error handling but for now it suffices to say that for most cases you can use a try catch block to handle errors inside an async function.

4.3 Async/Await Inside Loops

Let's say you need to perform a set of operations on a multiple local files. Your initial intuition might be use to use a looping mechanism like the forEach method:

```js
const files = ['./a.txt', './b.txt', './c.txt'];
files.forEach(file => {
  const r1 = await task1(file);
  const r2 = await task2(r1);
});
```

There are two issues with the code above:

1. The anonymous function passed to forEach is not marked async, so we can't use the await operator

2. Even if we made the anonymous function `async`, the `forEach` method wouldn't wait for all the tasks to be finished

Instead of the `forEach` method, we have two options that would work:

1. c-style for loop

```
async function main() {
  const files = ['./a.txt', './b.txt', './c.txt'];
  for (let i = 0; i<files.length; i++) {
    const r1 = await task1(files[i]);
    const r2 = await task2(r1);
  }
  return 'done';
}
```

2. `for of` loop

```
async function main() {
  const files = ['./a.txt', './b.txt', './c.txt'];
  for (const file of files) {
    const r1 = await task1(file);
    const r2 = await task2(r1);
  }
  return 'done';
}
```

The downside of the above approaches is that we won't be able to run the tasks concurrently, even though each tasks is asynchronous. For example, if the first file is huge, but the last file is very small, the function is going to be paused until all the operations on the first file is finished. A more efficient approach would be to define each operation as a promise and then process them all using the `Promise.all` method:

```
const files = ['./a.txt', './b.txt', './c.txt'];

async function operation(f) {
  const r1 = await task1(f);
  const r2 = await task2(r1);
  return r2;
```

```
7   }

8

9   const tasksPromises = files.map(operation);

10

11  Promise.all(tasksPromises)
12      .then(r => console.log(r))
13      .catch(e => console.log(e))
14      .then(_ => console.log('all done'));
```

In the snippet above, we define an async function that performs the two tasks in the order
that we like. Then we make an array of promises using the map method. Finally, we process
the promises using the `Promise.all` method. Note that the promises will be resolved in
different order, but the tasks in the `operation` function will be done in the order that we
wanted. You can take a look at an actual example in the code folder of the book's repo at
`code/async-await/loop/main.js`.